For my daughter and son,
Carolyn and Matthew:

Poetry Incarnate

AS I BREATHE ~ POETRY OF NATURE
Copyright © 2001 by Suzan Chamberlayne

Prana Publishing, Post Office Box 473, Eastsound, WA 98245-0473

ISBN 0-9710336-0-9
Library of Congress Control Number: 2001117039
First Edition

As I Breathe

Poetry of Nature

by
Suzan Chamberlayne

Illustrations by Jaqueline Rudd

Prana Publishing
Orcas Island, Washington

CONTENTS

ILLUSTRATIONS

PREFACE

September 8, 2000 marked the ten year anniversary of my arrival and first experience of *coming home* to Orcas Island. This collection of poems serves to commemorate that occasion and honor the Nature which inspired them. I feel strongly that no matter what our spiritual orientation, the truth remains that the kinder and more reverent we are to Nature, the finer the gifts we receive from her.

The first poem in this book, "Quantum Dance Partner," expresses the essence of my philosophy of life. Just as quantum physics now acknowledges an interrelationship between even the tiniest of particles, I see all of creation as interconnected and interdependent. I offer this book as my way of sharing the connection and joy I find in Nature.

Suzan Chamberlayne
April, 2001

PERSONAL ACKNOWLEDGMENTS

My father died at 86; my great nephew, at age 3; and I came close in the mid 1970's. Because we rarely know how long we have to express our gratitude, creating possible occasions to do so seems to me both appropriate and wise. Here is my such opportunity!

I thank my parents for giving me the gifts of breath, spirit and a good foundation; my children for helping me appreciate the gift of life.

Blessed with a multitude of *teachers* ~ family, friends, and professionals ~ yet unable to name many of them here, I express heartfelt gratitude to you all.

My appreciation extends from Mrs. Catherine Wheatley, Mrs. Pearl Norcross and Mrs. Letty Rogers, my language arts teachers at Holton-Arms School, in Washington, D.C.; to my first college professor, Dr. Janice Cole, who encouraged me to major in English; and, latterly, Professor Ed Rivers, at the University of Colorado, who in the 1990's taught me to break some of the rules of writing that I had spent so many years learning!

I thank my once-husband, Richard Chamberlayne, who nick-named me *Emily*; later-partner, Sid Copeland; as well as good friend, Gayle Weiss ~ all of whom blessed me with, and have taught me so much about love, kindness and joy.

Thank you, Susan Rosewell-Jackson, PhD, for your Jungian and Nature-loving approach to assisting my developing consciousness, compassion and trust; for helping so many move from a past into a future with a present.

x

Thank you, fellow-poet Bill Urschel, for over a decade of sharing both poetry and friendship. If it were not for your encouragement, this book might never have come to be.

I thank my friend, Jessica Spring, for always being supportive of my writing and whose own long letters provided a lifeline from across the Pacific in the 1990's.

Thank you, Aaron McKinnon for your shamanic way of opening doors to other dimensions.

Thanks to Ron Baer for your patient and generous assistance with the computer; and to Patty Johnson and *The Easy Writers*, for helpful editing advice.

Thank you, Andrea Hendrick, for referring me to Jackie, as well as for your kind, helpful assistance with the design process.

Alleluia for Jackie Rudd and her ability to transform words into images! Your beautiful spirit graced production of this book as much as your talent as a gifted artist.

I thank the Nature and Community of Orcas Island for providing such a nurturing environment to call *home*. My gratitude especially goes to a particular old-growth Douglas Fir near Doe Bay who intitiated me with one of the most significant experiences of my life.

Suzan Chamberlayne
April, 2001

Poetry of Nature

QUANTUM DANCE PARTNER

A single hair is dancing
On my sleeve.
Watching, gives it life,
As I breathe.

And if I laugh,
It twirls about,
Like I've given the cue
For stepping out!

We share the joy of reflection,
That hair and me.

THE COVE

A beached whale of a log
Lies massive,
Battered, but still.

Its big knot eye
Watches me
As my steps
Press the sand
In passing.

GLIMPSES

I

Water-reflected sunlight
Shimmers across dark brown bark
Like northern lights
Across a Canadian night sky.

II

Occasional rocks and roots
May trip me on my path.
'Tho sometimes stumbling,
I never completely fall.

III

Multitudes of fairies
Flicker across the sound,
Skimming the surface,
Thanks to this bright, waxing moon!

IV

Nettles refrain their sting
As I stay to the way
And sing their praises
For welcoming the butterflies.

V

Sleeping seahorses top unfurled ferns,
Unawakened by my soft step
In this sea of green
And brown forest floor.

ON THE SHORE

Tree woman . . .
Gnarled knee pressing beached boulders,
Barked pregnant belly hanging above
The impudent, slapping tide . . .
Hungers for the Father.

MESSAGE FROM THE BEACH

I sense the mystery
Of that cool white band
Encircling this dark stone:
The halo of a Nature Spirit
Slipped and lodged there
Forming a permanent reminder
Of the impossibility of imperfection.

Firm promise of holiness
Visually resounds from this
Ring of hope and glory.

REVERENCE

The cacophany of morning songbirds
Pauses . . .

As if all must attend,
In a moment of respect,

While the great Geese
Bark their dominance
Across a changing-season sky.

They wing above . . .
    Then are gone.

        Soon voices of robin and wren
        Resume . . .
        As if never their silence.

TURNING TIDE

Low tide whisper
Of the beach
Urges me on;
Siren's song.

Nature's treasures
Lure me
From rock to sand,
Around the strand.

Coaxed by loon's wail,
Eagle's flight,
I lose sight
Of my way
As the bay
Closes in.

High tide
Halts my stride!

Facing rock wall
    rising before me
I fully consider hope
    of walking on water.

SUN SHOWERS

Sometimes, when Sky
Cannot make up her mind
Whether to laugh or to cry,
She pours sun through rain,
Echoing a crazy note.

Simultaneously showering
Wet and wonder;
She sparkles with the laughter
Of God's joke.

MEETING THE SKY

Perched on a rock, up high
By the wellspring of creation,
I still expect to find the familiar.

When will I be weaned?
Learn to run up a beam of light
That dips into the night of the forest?
Or mount madrona's twisting trunk,
To taste the tip-top-most leaves,
Then swallow great gulps of cloud?

When will I fully know
What my senses see . . .
Truly discover Thee in me?

LUNA'S LURE

It's night now. Dark,
With a balloon moon
Teasing me to try
To soar that high.

Telling me tales
With lost lyrics,
Forgotten memories,
Recalled refrains.

Echoes through these hollow halls
Call me to fly –
To soar as high
As a balloon moon.

SACRED SOLITUDE

A solitary moth
Flutters up my windowpane,
Seeker of the light.

My solitary heart
Conjures up its pain,
Lost in the night.

Alone once again,
I smile away shadows
With a sigh on a prayer.

LETTING GO

I hear your breath
Inflate the world.
Then sigh release of it.
All's just that simple!

ALMOST-NEW

A sliver of a shining cradle
Hangs above night's horizon,
Ready to rock a baby star
Not far from lightyears away
Of play and promises —
Ready to wish upon itself.

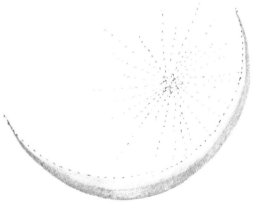

LOST WORDS

Fireflies flit in the night.

Are they a trick of light
On the periphery of my vision?

I reach for my pen,
Hoping to trap them with ink,

But they evaporate,
Leaving me

Alone in the dark,
Clutching an empty page.

REFLECTIONS

Sitting in lamplight
That washes my easy chair,
Looking toward dark night
Beyond my window there,

I wonder:
"Who is she . . .
That woman peering back at me?"

She watches me watching me
And we wonder.

MUTUAL PRESENCE

I walked the beach tonight,
Finding footholds and favorites,
Hard rocks beneath
Soft soles.

Of a dozen deer feasting
Fresh, green shoots nearby,
Only one stopped to witness me witness
Soft souls.

LIFE'S MIRROR

From the boat I watch
The nature of water
Ever shifting:
Here rippled peaks
Pop up in agitation . . .
There a patch of peace,
Smooth as glass;
Enigmatic change.

SIGNS

Flock of blackbirds
Scattered on red rooftop,
Like tealeaves at the bottom
Of a Chinese cup,
Wait to be read.

They wait to tell
My future, my fortune;
To share the secret
Of my life.

Then scatter to the sky
As though they'd never been,
Nor I.

MISLED

Sirius, the Dog Star, drew me to you
That *dog days of summer* night.

As bright as a little moon,
That trickster led me to your stable door
Like the star wise men followed.

But I, Unwise Woman,
Did not see the difference.

GRACE

A gift from my cat:
Several strands of fur
Left on the coverlet,
So that, as I breathe,
I might see them dance
In joyous celebration
Of my life!

WITH THE GODS

Though the edges are steep,
Looking down
On rocky beaches below,
I feel no fear of falling;

There is no threat
Here on Olympus.

Treescapes

I

Fallen fir,
Your dark-streaked trunk
And skeleton boughs,
Tell stories of another day,
Once upon a time,
When wild winds howled,
Cruel lightening struck,
And a sobbing sky
Wet this world so harshly
The ground could no longer
Hold you.

II

In this rich brown
Castle mound,
Moss-covered fortress
For lichen, beetles, bugs,
Echoes of an ancestor
Sprout forth as infant firs.

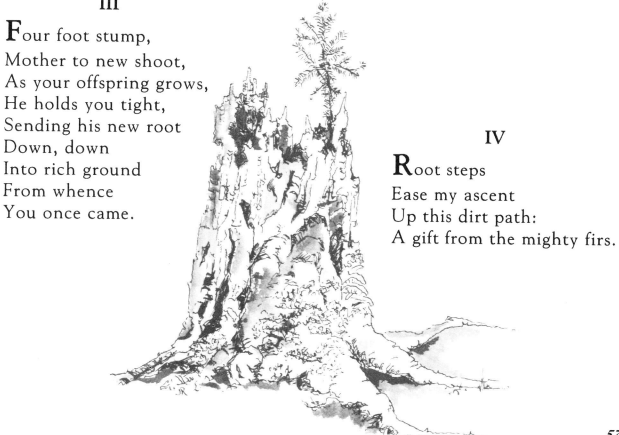

III

Four foot stump,
Mother to new shoot,
As your offspring grows,
He holds you tight,
Sending his new root
Down, down
Into rich ground
From whence
You once came.

IV

Root steps
Ease my ascent
Up this dirt path:
A gift from the mighty firs.

MATING SEASON

Springtime's double-duck
Stirs the pond.

Top tail wagging,
Forward head dipping ~
Fast, smooth glide
Through the watery ecstacy:

Dance of life's continuance.

SPRING SIGNS

I

Mosquito winging
Through cool, moist air:
Harbinger of summer's
Close chase.

II

No longer needing
Winter's weighty wrap,
I step lightly this path
To the compost,
Bearing gifts
For raccoon and rat.

III

Whispering apologies
To unwelcome ants,
I spring clean
My little cabin in the woods.

SUMMER SUNRISE

Like pre-symphony tuning,
Nature's harmony arises
From the cacophany.
Songbirds warm the morning chill
As they joyfully call
To come witness
Dawn of a miracle!

I heed their summons;
Pedal into the glow.
Breeze strokes my hair
As by a mother's palm;
Touches my lips
Like a magic wand;

Caresses my face,
Emanating joy;
Shares the secret:
We are truly blessed!

Prior to the Fourth of July

Full moon highlights summer gardens.
Clouds echo dropped tulip petals,
Faded lilacs' paling purple.

Waves of white hawthorne
Spray across our island, while
Clematis and iris wash her
In colorful explosions:

Nature's own pyrotechnic displays.

LESSONING FROM NATURE

Fine strands of web dust my cheek,
Tickle my awareness, saying I am the first
Along this path today.

Sleeping seahorses top unfurled ferns,
Unawakened by my soft step
In this sea of green and brown forest floor.

Stars already sparkle,
Line the path with flowery bursts
Amid latifolia leaves and grasses.

Nettles refrain their sting
As I stay the way and sing their praises
For welcoming butterflies.

Pithy, pregnant fir stretches her round belly
Into the trail, inviting me
To feel the stirrings of her womb.

Twits and twills spill from
The feathered guardians of her branches,
With splashes of sound and flutter.

Suddenly, loud, angry screams
From a sea plane ravage the peace;
Rip through these gentle woods.

But I, alone, am shattered.
The trees still stand as strong and tall
In their wise acceptance.

No leaf quivers. No lighted patches
Of bright green fade in the presumed intrusion.
All remains calm . . . except my mind.

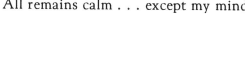

SYNESTHESIA?

He once told me,
"No one wants to hear
How great things go for you."

Suspecting he may have been right,
I grieve that I cannot share
This utter joy!

PERENNIAL CURE

Daisies cascade down a garden bank,
Overflow stone walls
Built by an aching back.

Daisies beam their bright glow
As white petal rays
Play on emerald chords.

Daisies brighten earth's brown,
Soften rigid rock,
Heal an aching heart.

REMINDERS

Pine needles dance
Sparkling web-threads,
Show me joy
Inherent in the wind
Of this cold, wet autumn.

Yellow leaves carpet
Ground all around,
Reflect cloud-hidden sun
To gently brighten
This gray day.

LATER

It's Fall.
Geese call.
You don't.

Gone are the heat
And comfort
Of summer.

LESSENING

How can it be,
This losing and finding?
What humble exaltation,
The wisdom of finally knowing nothing.

HONORING

I curl into myself;
A bow from the belly
Greeting your greatness
With *namaste*.

LUNA

Is there really a man in the moon?

Or is she virginal, alone,
Unfettered, unknown?

Is that what assures
She shines so bright?

Or is it a plight, she knows
Not her solitude, her beauty?

Autumn Echoes

Madrona's peeling paper
Whispers a message . . .
Leaves me
Fearing the Fall,
As lengthening shadows
Spread across my mind.

THAT RAINY MONDAY ON LOPEZ

After elevenses,
We sit until two,
Claiming our corner
Of *Love Dog Café*.

Curled on couch and chair,
We share Rumi,
In that room with a view
Of deep red laurel leaves,
Weathered split rails
And Fisherman's Bay.

Together, we partake
An apt appetizer:
Word and photo portraits
Of the models we choose
For later years.
Old Age Is Not For Sissies,
The title page declares.
We taste laughter and love
Served from its binding.

Then, appetites whetted,
We savor Charlotte's garden greens
And pumpkin pie at a table for two
Near the window.

By the time we depart,
We truly understand papa's words:
"Perfection or something better!"

WISHES ON THE WATER

Mermaids ~ ocean angels,
Guardians of the gate
To Deepest Mind ~
Initiate me.

Baptize my thoughts;
Help them drift and float,
Become a boat
To transport my body

Back to quiet waters.

ULTIMATE FOUNTAIN

Words flow
From the spigot of You
Through dry darkness
Moistening all that's parched.

IN THY IMAGE

Is that You
The glue holding
It all together?
The pen writing
The poem?
The fingers finding keys
To our harmony?

BELOVED

If The Creator be my new lover,
How will I flirt?

Why toss tresses
When I can throw a pot?

Color on canvas will woo
Finer than painted cheeks.

We'll stay up late on dates,
Star-gazing, moon-bathing,

Then greet dawn without yawns,
Proving poetry our lovesong.

HANGING ON

Savor the stirrings
As a last, late wisp of wisteria
Delicately splashes purple
Across yellowing leaves
And jade green spines.
Thick, old, twisted
Woody vines
Hold secrets
Older than our knowing.

COMMUNION

In this sanctuary,
I hear visions, see songs,
While waves of light
Dance through darkness,
Waves of wet stroke desert sand.

Once again, I am
The grain, the drop
Of Thee.

DECEMBER STORM

For days, the wind
Moaned and screamed,
Slashed and scarred
With cruel, icy tentacles.

We watched it whip white-capped crests
Across the surface of a once-still pond
Until the water — hardened
By the onslaught
Of its relentless oppressor —
Could no longer be moved.

YEAR'S END

Cascade Falls,
After snow and so much rain,
Sprays again
As opalescent as fairy wings.

She flings her flow
Over the edge
In joyous celebration.
Bright white highlights
Washed greens, burnished browns.

Hypnotic plunge:
Action, change, constancy
Wear away clay and stone,
This last day of the year.

Beyond
MADRONA POINT

Ghost Trees crown the point,
Sun bleached and salt sprayed,
Reflecting moonlight;
Beacon for unsettled souls
Lost at sea.

Wood pale and parched,
Like bare bones
Washed upon the shore
In times past.
Sailors' widows, long gone
To their own graves on land,
No longer wait or wonder,
"Will he come home?".
No hand now clasps a locket;
No honing heart drops
A memory with a tear.

Nothing remains except . . .
Ghost trees on the shore,
Sun bleached, salt sprayed,
Reflecting moonlight.

Under the Skylight

Ravaged by the man in the moon
I melt into my sighs

Inflated with in-breath
Float above my bed

Relaxed by each exhale
Sink deep into pillow and pad

Then dance out the other side
Of my dreams ~ follow them home

Devoid of armies or altars
Purpose or pitfalls

In love with divinity I merge
With Ultimate Peaceful Passion

A NEW DAY

This morning, a breath of fresh air
~ more of a prayer than a breeze ~
slipped through
my bedroom curtain and,
like an impatient lover,
caressed me awake.

Ah, what fortune, this other
lover's kiss of grace,
arousing a stretch of joy,
as I rub my eyes open
to a new view
of bounteous blessings!

PLACE OF GRACE

Here in the woods,
Bramble greets flowering bush
As easy as sky.

Deadened branch,
Laden with lichen and moss,
Adds as much to the whole
As the power green of fir,
Or soft-draping cedar bough.

Rotting log,
As fine a fundament
As seed pods.

In this place of grace,
All's essential . . .
Gives its gift . . .
Maintains nurturing balance.

On the isle of healing waters,
With the currents all around her,
Here the Deer Guide led her downward.
Here it called to her *come home.*

Under skies of healing rainfall,
With the showers cleansing daily,
Here the Eagle raised her upward.
Here it called to her *come home.*

In the woods of deepest meaning,
With the Tree of Ancient Knowledge,
Here Earth Mother cradled Layla.
Here it lulled her to *come home.*

Through the light of understanding,
With her mission clearly shown her,
Here the Shaman healed her brethren;
Here she helped them to *come home.*

LAYLA'S CHANT

LEVITATION

Sometimes this vaulted ceiling
Fills with vacuum ～
Emptiness draws me up.

Wafted by the beat of invisible wings,
Maybe lifted by invisable strings,
I rise to meet It

And enter the ecstacy
Of full nothingness ～
Magnificent paradox.

ECHOES OF SILENCE

The sound of one dry leaf
Scurrying across my path
Halts.

We listen,
That leaf and I.

Thin dragonflies
Bump blades of grass
But never shatter the silence.

Just the echo of one dry leaf
Haunts my memory.

One dry leaf.

CO-CREATION

Whether we paint or pot,
Write or render,
Tapping our creative aspect
Sends a Morse-like message
Honoring our godhead
And heart.

Fragments carried:
Imprinted chicks, peeping
Accrued questions through
Mind's hollow hallways.

Sneaking up back stairs,
Sliding down split hairs,
Until laughter
Recognizes folly.

Electric spaces fill brain, being;
Tease that live wire,
Charged with a day done
Yet going on.

Until fire fed with breath
Finally makes peace
With Passion
In the fullness
Of an empty space.

VALUED VOID

QUIET MOMENT

I simply stop.
Sit still until
My mind
Cascades clear,
Washes thought away,
To finally float free
On a sea of silence.

Buddha under the Bodhi,
Jesus at Gethsemame,
Mohammad in his cave,
Gandhi on the ground:

All knew the power
Of simply sitting still.

LIFE'S SAVORING

Nature's condiments,
Sprinkled on my days,
Add flavor to the feast
Of my life.

01-01-01

Tea and toast
By an alder fire.

Cinnamon and cloves simmer
In an old iron pot.

Memories and musings
Await words.

This moment meets
A new day, new year.

MY FRIEND

Clouds scribbling messages
Across the hazy glow
Of an almost-full moon
Remind me of one June and you.

Sharing smoke and delight
That moonlit night,
In your old red Rambler,
You introduced me to
The best view.

From Crescent Beach we watched
That amorous man in the moon
Rise above Eagle Ridge,
To greet his waving mate,
Reflected in the bay below.

Was that your way of saying
Good-bye, long before you died?
I miss how you made moments . . .
Moments that last forever.

In memory of Heidrun Uhrmann Badgley

Dusk du Jour

Air, fragrant with fir-scent after rain,
Calls us down to the harbor
In time to see salmon-colored clouds
Leap from the bay
To taste the delicious glow
Of today's setting sun.

WELCOME HOME

God came home today.
Or was it I who was away?

Now Love lays out my heart
Like a welcome mat.

GIFT OF MORTALITY-CONSCIOUSNESS

So many sacred moments
Could be my last.

Yet here's another,
Just knowing it was not!

MADRONA IN GLORY

Madrona knows she shows
Better in the sun.
Stretching sienna-skinned limbs
Out over the edge,
She listens to a loon.

Waves, washing rocks on the bank,
Reflect her orange hue
Like a tossed message
To stones and starfish below.

She peels curls of paper secrets
To allow the softness of her
Hidden bark to shine.
Madrona shows she knows.

Suzan Chamberlayne, the poet, lives with her black cat, white dog and 80 house plants on Orcas Island, in the San Juans of Washington State.

Jaqueline Rudd, the illustrator, is a watercolor artist who makes her home on Orcas Island.

Prana Publishing
P.O. Box 473
Eastsound, WA 98245-0473
(360) 376-3025

To Order **As I Breathe** - **Poetry of Nature**

Please Complete the Form Below
and Mail With Check or Money Order to:

℘ PRANA PUBLISHING

P.O. Box 473, Eastsound, WA 98245-0473

NAME: _____ PHONE: _____

ADDRESS: _____

CITY: _____ STATE: _____ ZIP CODE: _____

NUMBER OF COPIES: _____ AMOUNT ENCLOSED: $ _____

Price per book: $12.95 U.S. or $18.95 Canadian
Plus Shipping & Handling: $4.00 for first book + $1.00 for each additional book

Or order by phone at (360) 376-3025